A Prelude to Love

Milan Ester

CONTENTS

PREFACE

The skimp on *rich* relationships is a longevity killer. We can be exorbitant about many things, but skimp on our relationships. We're so worth it though. Be exorbitant about you. Let him be gushing about you, and be excessive about him. No, no. We don't have to be filthy rich financially to be extravagant about him. Nor is exorbitance about arrogance. If you can gush about him more next year than last, it's a step in a good love direction. It's worth the dig a little deeper to know that we can sustain the gush before taking the love plunge. Sometimes, what maintains happiness to fulfilment gets lost in our day-to-days, but decadent love is stronger. What makes the sexy honey he dated become more lackluster? What makes him lose his appeal?

Who's that into you that they would give anything to discover what makes you the most valuable person on earth? Yes, and still find you *that* intriguing, or much more, if you had a million years from now.

What are you like? What is she about? One of the things about love is it can make anything beautiful, but if we don't give love a chance, we miss experiencing it for what it is. If we don't know what it is, we go blindly into something for some reason that may not be love. A weekend of truffles may be more about his motives than your heart. If her attraction is about your money, what do you have?

A Prelude to Love is a very practical observation of our love things, intended to be provocative enough to make us think, at least. Love being the complete package that it is, is sometimes best expressed more comparatively. So, while *A Prelude to Love* is straight-up chitchat about our love things, occasionally we try to get to our rich love destination using a figurative approach.

Challenge you to be a better lover. You may be surprised that you are truly suave, debonair and irresistible!

YOUR LOVE LANGUANGE

Danielle meticulously executed her entire repertoire – princess pamper, lusty lingerie, in the mood. Now, she stands in the perfect spot, and strikes Kevin's favorite pose just before he walks in with the bushel of roses for her. He opens the door, senses her, and looks from pampered pedicure in seductive stilettos to her sexiness. He drops the roses, and everything else… Kisses, fondles and foreplay later, they say love by making love.

Say love. Go ahead… Express it verbally, physically, or do your best love thing. Say it with the best sex ever, a box of chocolates, lavish gifts,… Or, you can say love verbally to him with "I love you", or a simple "Hey Sexy!" What does he hear? What does she hear when you say love? Maybe, he hears love. Perhaps she hears, "You think I'm sexy". It is commendable to try to express love to someone. It is most effective if what we express really is love. Who gets to decide what love is and is not, though?

We hear love to be *that:* perhaps, a sex, money or emotional thing. What do we perceive love to be? Relationships and families change based on *perceptions* of love.

When the sex changes, love does not. If money comes or goes, love still remains constant. Unstable economies and markets do not affect love's position. Love is not tied up in the money, politics, feelings, nor the sex. It is an independent that maintains constant position irrelevant of our sways. So, what do we have? If love is a constant, and we keep falling in and out of it, what exactly is happening? And why are we falling? From where? *Was* that love? And, if indeed "love is power", it should have some capacity to hold us steady and prevent us from falling out of it.

Love has power, but so does our will. Love Ambiguous says, "Hold me, Love!", but fights love all the way to the next relationship. Love still holds her while she fights, whether she is falling from love, already hit the ground running from love, or wherever she is.   As much as we may want love to hold us, if our will to do something else overrules, the will trumps love's efforts; not love, love opportunities.

So is it the "people change" argument that explains our fickles? Perhaps. Isn't it more beneficial to invest in something that is stable instead of love perceptions that may fold? When do we step away from our perceptions and consider relevant, sexy love?

Most of us really want love, but we continue to manufacture humanity incapable of giving and receiving real love. The clear receiver so hears the voice of love that it is influenced to love, give love, and move others in the direction of love. A broken or defective heart cannot possibly contain a love we want, function as it should, nor can it give what it does not possess.

What does anyone hear at your interpretation of love? Is it the way you say love or what she hears? Maybe what you said is what you *think* love is. We ask too much of the imperfect heart when we request or demand that it love like anything more than it can. Some of us are too busy to hear. It is a great world where we can flurry in the busyness and still hear unmistakably the voice of love enough to express it precisely. Ultimately, she wants him to hear distinctively well because her expression is true, and has the power to influence well: so does he.

It is blatantly clear, based on divorce rates, separation statistics, quality of relationships and stressful break-ups, that most of us have missed the boat on the love thing. Perhaps, it's time to do something other than our love views.   It is futility to think that human efforts will not sometimes fail in expressing love. But, what a complete waste to not discover some aspect of the extreme phenomenon enough to live a complete success.

MISRATED: SEX IN THE LOVE GAME

As sexy as the sex is, consider sex that comes from hearts that have tapped love! Oh, yeah! Unfettered! Luxurious! 'Tis boom sex! Sex as an expression of rich love is on the other side of sex to *get* love. Well, he may be about more than the sex. It's a start, but can he go there? To the love place. Can she be about love if it's all about the money or security? How willing is he to approach love or turn in the direction of love?

Some of the most misleading mistakes are assuming that sex is love, can lead to love or determines how love will play out. Sexing to see if love is worth it is common. Too many people get so hung up on the sex, love becomes a figment. And sex can make love things fuzzy… Is she capable of going past the sex? Is he? We sometimes start what we do not want.

If you're not vested in love, most likely, he will not be if sex is really all he wants. People aren't giving heart for sex. Sex is a casual thing for many relationships. Anyone can have sex or try to have sex. Where's the heart? This is an inherent problem with sexing and relationships. If it's about sex for him, then it will not be about you to the extent of love. Yes, he may *do* "for you", but the motivation will be the sex. Again, you've been slighted, and that's not being excessive about you. It's about the sex. Can it *become* about you? Possibly. Your relationship becoming about you has to do (in part) with if he's gone to the depths of what makes his heart beat so, or not.

Most of us are inclined to be more on the "about-me" side. The devout coffee-lover couldn't even give up the morning coffee if the industry were on the brink of extinction and one morning a week without a cup could save it. It takes a severe blackout for the couch potato to miss an episode, and he only misses the show if every television in a 50-mile radius is not showing. What's the point?

Just as we wouldn't sacrifice a cup of coffee, an episode or whatever our "fix", we bring the same approaches to our relationships. If we don't love him or her like that, then it is best to not envelop him or her in our love shenanigans. So, if we are not in it for love, and that is what he wants, simply put, leave him alone. But what about someone who starts out with ulterior motives, but changes somewhere in the relationship game. It does happen, but it is a chance.

Love being an independent "principle" works with certain terms in place. We may say, love has terms. And sexing is not really one of them. It's quite the "fringe benefit" and serves so many luxe purposes, but it is not love. Just as the earth has laws, like gravity, by which it works, so does love. If we do not believe gravity, we still fall if we jump from some height. Gravity works, whether we're sold on it or not. Love works. The principles of love work. And while sex is not a principle of love, per se, it can be a most sexy result of it. What a boom sex it is, though, with sexy love!

Our drivers to *do* "love" are very various. For some, our attempt at love is fear. For others, it's a fad or tradition. People get married and have a family, so we do. "Don't really love him like that" or her, but "don't want to be alone for the rest of my life", … They may just be good enough. So we do the marriage thing. When we can't give up the game for her, or forego chips and crackers in bed for him, how could we possibly have love, when inherent in love is some ability to defer? Most of us have something: maybe even a little love, but that's all. Yes, it is a start.

It may be fair to resolve that love has degrees. To address love, it may be most productive to discuss a highest degree. If at least we can deliberately *aspire* to love's highest degree, that is significant progress. If you cannot give up a smokes for her, that is where you are. Where do you want to be in the love "game"? Relationally, it is critical to establish such foundationals before taking a plunge.

Whatever level of love, there are associated terms. If you cannot both agree to terms of approaching love, that is, at least, an impediment. Love relationships require at least two people working it out together. He golfs after work and that's the way it is. If you can't find a hobby to bide your time, it's best to save your heart, your time and your money if the golf bothers you *that* much. You should probably reconsider the grand wedding until you can work out the golf. He's not quite there. Would it matter if he met her naked and ready for out-of-this-world hot sex at 6 p.m. on the dot? If he rushes out after the high to the golf game, that's more antagonizing than him being married to the game. If the game is that important or more important, consider that there could be an inherent and fundamental dilemma in the heart of him irrelevant of you. It's not about twenty minutes nor an hour of hot sex. It is more productive to find out what's ticking in him. Why should it be okay with you?

If love is the quest, then it is necessary to go to heart places. Establish if you're in it for love, formalities or other. Love is worth it. Where does she want to go? Do you want to go there? If you cannot both agree to some terms of approaching love, even with professional help, que sera *may* be the game: at least, for now.

INFLUENCE

Most of us can do the pleasure directive. If we don't know how to perform, we can learn. There is a mass wealth of info on how to sex, be sexy, attract and be attractive. And most of us are motivated to master the feel good because it *feels* good. Physiological, psychological and heart semantics, though? Love is supposed to be fun and freedom and pleasureful. Oui, oui. How about if we talk about the *feel*-good part of love? The feel-good is so extremely and disproportionately emphasized, that most of us think that is what love is.

How much we cooperate with love determines how much we benefit from it. To say "love hurts", automatically causes disinterest. Does love hurt? Pain can be relative. We can associate anything with pain, if we don't want to do it. It's like the toddler with the tummy ache every time it's dinnertime. Her tummy never hurts when it's time for desserts and treats. All things being equal, the phantom pain over broccoli and potatoes is really about the less palatably appealing, but nourishing, part of her daily diet that does not touch her sweet tooth.

There are fundamentals in becoming a good lover. Lover: a master at love (not "lover" as in lover-boy or sex toy, as we know it). If we have no desire to adapt to love's ways, we've made our choice to remain mediocre lovers, below average or alone. Yes, alone is not necessarily bad, but for some reason, most of us aspire to have the right person in our world. Being a good lover is not for the faint of heart. For the art of mastering oneself is another one of the lost arts. Who are you? Inside. Nevermind our bank or lack thereof. Our professional rung on the ladder of corporate, our suave, and debonair aside. Inside, who are you? If we are unable to go there, it is so limited where we can go in becoming good lovers. If we want to become, we must go inside.

Who wants to cooperate with anything else given our daily mandatory matters? A cooperative is just that: the necessity to co-operate. We're already sighing with sudden bouts of severe fatigue! Anyone can muster strength from somewhere after an iron man to perform sexual feats if they really wanted to. But the very thought of going to the us inside that needs fixing to create, foster and accommodate the art of good lover, can suck the enthusiasm right out of us.

It's worth it! Cooperating with love is so worth it. We've all done at least one thing we had absolutely no interest in doing, but we pulled up the bootstraps, and did it anyway, because it was good for us. Mastering the art of good love is good for you. In what way, you ask? One, love is the great influencer. It's not limited to just relationals and sex associations. The influencer directs hearts, nations, economies and organizations.

There are millions of long-legged sexy beauties slinking the runways and streets of New York, Paris, and wherever. Who and what attracts a lover? If indeed million dollar legs and flawless skin could cut it, more of such appealing superficials would also suffice in the great relationship category. Even the ones that seem to last, how *did* they last? How are they holding up? We see what may be displayed. What is happening behind the scenes in relationships? Are we really doing well or just keeping it together? Who is fronting and who really has something? (Fronting: putting up a façade.) Who cares? Why should we care what and if *they* have something?

Living deliberately is max living. It's not so much that we can't all live this way. Most of us settle for the journey that makes the most sense to our limited capacity. Smarts and intelligentsia does not mean that she lives her max potential. And as much as max living is available to all of us, a rare few embrace it. The statistics depicting the rarity of living love are seen in the predicaments of the human experience. Kudos to our rare subset who start well, progress well and have astounding relationships. It is devastating to see the relational dynamics, insecurities and dysfunction that seem to be more influential. It is one thing for such cycles to prevail in us only. If we could possibly keep it that way - affecting only oneself – love deficiency would eat only *us* alive, instead of spreading like the epidemic that it is to the wider human race.

Politics is not really just politics, neither is economy just economics. Decisions get made by men and women who are good, bad or mediocre lovers. How does love walk the halls of governments and swing the markets? By the hearts and bent of our leaders and ourselves. We create our themes. If it is justice, love, beauty then that is what we have. If injustice and corruption, then we live wading through the results. If love is only about good or bad sex, his or her bank, or the likelihood to afford success in the next five years, then it is limited to our perceptions. At the point that we can perceive love to be the universal influencer that it is, we have a place of embarkation on the journey of love that can produce the best lovers.

HEART TRAINER

Buff body works the physique to the desired result. Healthier buff works the inside too. He who pumps iron, builds muscle, strengthens, and tones. He who trains the heart, commands the life. Imagine if we trained our hearts with the same zeal as we pump up! It is doubtful that we arrive to anywhere on our journeys without at least one heart shaper. Our *response* to the shapers on the way contribute to the bent of our heart.

As children, we are more impressionable by our circle of influences. By the time we can decide a bent, the heart has developed a mind and a will of its own. We still have the power, though, to respond based on better principles. If we continue to respond from the language of an inequitably impressioned heart, we cannot possibly hope to become the best lovers.

Are we most trained by relationships, material wealth, environment or other? Some elements of these play a role in our perspectives. We love ourselves enough for a pedicure, a day at the spa or the new Rolex. But do we love us enough to address our less displayable, but more influential, elements?

Whatever your heart trainer, the heart can be redirected to a good bent. Most of us opt out. To effectively talk love is to address oneself first, and go beyond pleasantries and niceties. Whole breeds whole relationships. It is fundamental to bring to the table of our affairs a good dose of healing. Heart lovers don't really care that they can front for the cameras, the boss, or the office. What speaks of our sincerity to have true love rests so much in our attitude to being whole. It is a call to address oneself. It is a demand on the self to be transparent. It is a journey worth taking.

So do we *not* approach love because we're not whole? Even when we are whole, we inevitably encounter challenges that threaten our wholeness. A basic requirement in attempting love is a willingness to sincerely lean towards becoming a good lover. Maybe little bitty steps are more feasible than leaps, but step in the right direction to get closer to the goal.

The heart that quits at the thought of confronting itself, needn't volunteer for any significant progress with love. Inherent in love is perseverance. Perseverance does not quit. It is not required to go the entire journey of becoming love in a few long strides. Becoming love can take a lifetime. It is important to stay the course. Unfortunately, too many of us cannot muster much to become love. Don't stay on the pier waving to poor, brave souls willing to take the journey to discover a most invaluable destination. Embark. First with yourself. If we can start with us, we have the basis to positively influence our families and friends, and our wider communities, with love. And yes, even another endearing heart can be influenced to increase its capacity to give, and receive, love.

The heart that learned to hate the oppressor slams its doors shut to any experience or encounter that resembles the oppressor, or promises to oppress. Do we continue to bring the heart to the doorstep of oppression or whatever our yesterdays? Or, do we find love's ways in dealing with the yesterdays? What are love's protocols for a heart trained by oppression? By grief? By abuse? By horror? By injustice? Some of the most indelible marks are made by negative experiences. Extract from it something of value, if you can, and go impact your world. One of the most beautiful things about love is its profound knowledge of the root systems of any heart and its effective finesse with any bent. So, bent-out-of-shape oppressor, abuser, and passive get trumped any day.

The open heart that remains free has no bitterness with which to respond to the onslaughts. This is the heart that regroups itself, gives love a chance and reopens the life to progress, and the possibilities of destiny. If your heart can direct itself to a higher resolve than hate, distrust, revenge, fear, unforgiveness or negativity, facilitate it. For these poison the life, and discolor the world. If yesterday has so overwhelmed the heart that it cannot possibly perceive of a higher resolve, wait.

Our hearts may not have to overcome the devastation of wars, plague, epidemic and abject poverty. The challengers of so many of our hearts reside in the injustices of basic emotional needs and other intangibles unmet (especially during childhood). Emotional, physical and sexual abuses and deviances, or deficits so impression the life. Many of our hearts get trained by absentee parenting, poor parental skills and neglect. And, it is not just depravity that trains the heart. Many a heart is trained by excess. The song of greed is quite the tune. And, money is such a top lure to a heart infatuated with it, evil is a piece of cake if evil is what it takes to have money.

It is futile to want endearing, and be a love debacle. It is one thing to be a debacle with sincere interest in being a lover. It is quite another to maintain resolutely love debacle, while expecting another to play our game. Love calls the debacle and the hopeful. Only the hearts that come stand a chance.

There is a very particular admiration for the heart that knows itself well enough to say, I'm not game for this or that. Most disheartening are hearts that continue to enlist another's on a journey to which it has no courage nor intention to go the destination, especially knowingly.

It is necessary to ask where will he take me or where is she going prior to embarkation. Where will this end? It is futility to ask such questions of a heart you do not trust, or will not learn to trust, for whatever reason. For distrust alone is a premise to leave the suitcases in the closet or under the bed. There is already a flag on the play. Even the most well-intentioned heart strays from the planned destination. Just because he promised to take you to Bliss, doesn't mean that he can. It is okay to sincerely try. Are you willing to regroup a failed attempt? ... Sometimes, again.

Take responsibility for yourself with the love journey. Typically, we have indicators to help us determine where a journey *may* end. Where did his other journeys end? What is her track record? No, past destinations don't necessarily decide today's journeys, but it may be vital to resolve what led to distasteful endings enough to get to some resemblance of bliss. If a fling is all you're looking for, by all means, go for fling-girl, or Mr. Extracurricular. But, the heart of love things requires a heart vested in love things. It is astounding the *desire* for "real love" compared to the *effort* we are willing to make to have it. Effort is not necessarily difficult. It is necessary.

It is critical for us to adapt, regroup, change and grow. The fact that there are "levels" of love, means there is always room to grow. It is not necessarily comfortable, but if we want more than we are receiving from love, more may be required from us.

Truth is a fundamental to grow love. Usually truth has to be presented tactfully. Why has your relationship changed? What is it about her that no longer works? What about him? Why is he not willing to consider your requests to become more? If he doesn't *say*, you may need to become deft at self-analysis. To say, I respect her too much to say *that* to her, is a step away from truth. And since truth is a fundamental for progress in becoming love, it is imperative to somehow communicate truthfully and effectively

with each other, and oneself. It may not even be about you.
Maybe it's about him or her. Are you committed enough for
significant-other-analysis to help her get where she needs to be? Is
she interested in going where you need her to be?

Love Ambiguous and Lover stalemated on their quest. Is it
permanent, temporary or needing intervention? Making permanent
decisions based on temporary snags can throw away a good thing.
Maybe, they need assistance. Should they walk away?

HE SAYS BREAD. SHE HEARS JAM.

He says bread. She hears sandwich. What's worse, is that he is adamant that all he means is bread, but it really *is* a sandwich. Some communication breakdowns *require* professional intervention. It is futility to try to convince her if she is completely sold on a position that is so ingrained, she sees the world through personal-colored glasses.

Fundamental to the art of communication is one of the humility sciences, listening. Being a listener takes deliberate effort, especially with our on-the-go lifestyles. Fundamentally, it is vital in communicating, to *prepare* the heart to *listen* - to the spoken and unspoken. If the subject matter is a heavy-weight, even more so. Nobody enjoys being pummeled with facts or opinions that do nothing for the ego, or our pride. If we consider the value of listening, usually what he is saying is worth something.

Listening is active - not just being *silent* when he is speaking. Good listening literally directs your heart, and mind, to hear what he is saying and process it, correctly. Being silent can be a listening trickster. For we can be silent, holding our own great and important points in our mind, so we don't forget while they "ramble on". If we do not hear, we did not listen, or may need clarification to comprehend. For one of the indicators of good listening is hearing so well, we understand. Did you understand what she said? Not your interpretation of what he said, but *what* he said. Do you understand enough to move you to act, with the correct action, if necessary?

Trace his heart. What *is* he saying if it is unclear? Ask questions. Good listening sometimes requires *"extracting"* from him what he is trying to say, but is unsuccessful saying it. If we know him, we would know how he communicates. There is a place of love where one knows another.

Communication is not always a spoken word. We communicate with our actions: sometimes more loudly than we do with our speech. Do we spend ourselves mind-reading, body-language decoding or following her mime? Does it help? Be certain that you read her accurately, and talk it through, if necessary.

To judge is to conclude. Judging says I have already formed an opinion based on some "evidence". Opinions are not necessarily factual. Facts aren't always the whole story, and some facts are based on limited knowledge. The opinionated is hampered by his own perspective that impedes his ability to listen with an open mind. Fighting for our position does not allow us to come to the table to listen effectively. We don't have to say we've already decided our position. It is sometimes clear if we have decided prior to listening by our display, and how we respond to *their* position.

Inherent in empathy is the ability to relate on a more profound level to someone else. It is limited how well we can relate to someone with which we have no bond. Some bonds are stronger than others. It is easier for us to empathize with those with whom we share similar or common experiences. Even if we don't share a similar experience, *sensitivity* fosters developing empathy. Case: He says, my dad worked all the time so we didn't spend time together. Go there! Responding with, I wish my Dad wasn't there (because he was not the ideal, nicely put), could be perceived as veering off-track instead of empathy. It's not easy to relate to someone wanting their Dad to be there when ours may have been a problem Dad, to whatever extent. Go through the heart of someone who didn't have quality time with a "good" Dad. It may be helpful to you to consider what it would have been like to have a quality Dad around. What physiological and psychological needs are provided for predominantly by a father? Research it. Study it if you don't know, and bring it to your communications. Yours and his. If an absentee-father child lacked protection, security, etcetera from Dad, how does not having such necessities affect him, or her? How does it affect *your* relationship? It is a major stride towards understanding to go there. Such practical steps, done right, are usually effective for creating a bond and improving communication. Understanding nurtures good relationship, and some of the groundwork necessary to empathize. Empathy has listened and heard, therefore it is able to communicate better.

They were burning bras in the 60s-70s, but there was more to the story than the picture presented. There usually is. What is the whole story being presented? Good communication goes behind the presentation to the whole story. Relationships go up in flames because she's not hearing him, and she's not speaking his language. Of course, she may not make sense: neither does he. We come from different worlds, backgrounds and scenarios. Relationships can be places of great new norms and worlds, however, if they go bust before we can make it great, we have another fragmented rope, or broken bridge. The world is no stronger with cut ropes dangling that are supposed to be unbreakable, and we cannot cross if bridges are broken.

Before we cut the ropes and burn the bridges, we may have to traverse his background, and her scenarios, with a heart that says, I will understand enough about her passion, about his, to be an effective lover! Talk it! Listen it! Hear it! Understand it! Change it, where necessary! …But love deeply enough to make it!

Make it great!

HEARTSCAPES

If your heart were a work of art, what would it be? And where is the artist in the process of completing your magnum opus? Does she even know what tools and supplies are required to start the piece?

The color of some of our hearts are so broken, some despairing, others dead, some lost. The hemorrhaging heart must be repaired to maintain and sustain life. For the most part, so many of us have little or no capacity to hold love, nor life. If you can see a picture of our hearts…

It's shocking that most of us have survived at all. Life can be atrocious and devastating. It can also be exquisitely grand. One of the noblest goals of love is to support a life that is exquisitely grand. 'Tis a heart most wonderfully rare that remains open after, and through, offensives. How do we do that? How do we transcend the yesterdays to approach becoming love?

Deep in the heart are the roots of living that have affected the life. And, as much as we have the power to live from a better perspective, we tend naturally to live from such places. We carry generations and ancestors, places and events. And we bring them to the table of love. If the wounds and pain did not lodge so deeply in our heart places, they wouldn't affect the work of art on our canvases, and we could easily shake off the surface things so that they would have no bearing on our soul. [Soul: simply put, life].

Sometimes it is necessary to change the heartscape. It *is* possible to adjust the heart. But real heart adjustments are root-sized. That's another reason why we have to go inside. We are usually overwhelmed by the extreme events and circumstances in our lives, but they have a way of *revealing* what is really inside. They also present the opportunity to work out what is inside. Anyone can skip with brisk and high steps through a great sound of symphonic orchestra where all is well and in their favor. How we respond when all is not well and in our favor, tells how much what is inside governs our lives. If we really want the epitome of love, we may need to get to where our roots show so that we can change them to what grows love.

Unearthing roots is very dirty business, and can be so uncomfortable. Love knows what we can handle, though. And if we cannot trust love to go there, we are only game for where we can go. Again, it's okay. Be willing to change your heartscape yourself, have it changed by…, or ensure it resembles a heart that can accommodate love.

Every day people lay their hearts down at the feet of someone to love it and keep it. Some attend the heart soiree, but never lay their hearts down. If her life so clearly paints a picture of her heart, why did you lay your heart there? What exactly did you see in his display that drew your heart to his feet? Do you know your own work of art? How did your tour de force-in- progress influence your decision to lay your heart at *her* feet?

What so occupies your heart? Can love fit in there? If there is no room for love, love gets overruled by whatever authority presides. Be deliberate about other authorities seated in love's space.

APPROACHING LOVE

If love knocked on your door, can you fly with it? It's quite funny. We do have it backwards. We think of it as finding love, or falling in love, or something having to do with us commanding love. If *love approaches you*, can you dance with love? As great as the dance with love can be, the parameters and steps are quite meticulous. Not difficult. Specific. Love's agenda is usually difficult to the heart that resists it.

If we want to approach a beautiful sexy "honey", it may be uncomfortable, but in order to approach her, we have to step in her direction. If you want to approach love, you have to step in love's direction. For the most part, most of us want to approach love on our terms. Love has terms. The terms are, for the most part, different from ours, but they are most powerful and beneficial. In fact, they benefit us more than our own terms. The only way to find out though is to embrace love. Embrace love: play its way, learn its game, and love!

The clichéd "love is complex" may not most accurately measure love's difficulty level. The complexities, or simplicity, of love is sometimes defined by the perspective of the hearts involved. It is most profound the level of selfishness in some of the human experience. Again, if we won't do the dishes for him or her, it's not because love is difficult as much as it is about something else – possibly, our lack of ability to consider another above ourselves. But isn't it love that requires us place another above ourselves?

Why is this difficult from our perspective when we have the ability in us to do it?

Lover that has adapted the mind to the principles of love, finds it most difficult to be about oneself first. And doing the dishes for her is actually a *pleasure*! So, it is most natural to be about another first. No, not necessarily to your detriment. This level of love is so powerful, Lover's needs and desires are fulfilled. Lover thinks and lives on a different playing field. Doing the dishes is only a placeholder for whatever we find it impossible to do for another, especially our love interests. And of course, illegal and harmful practices aside, what can you do for him? What can you do for her?

Selfishness may be a little more than a comfort zone thing. But let's start there. Is it that uncomfortable to do something for another? Well, let's be polite and say, it's an indication of our love metric. You only love him so much. Where do you want to go? Do you at least have your head, heart and will turned in the direction of being a better lover? If adjusting is not your thing, then it is limited how much more love you can expect to contain. Do we change for him? Shouldn't we just love and be loved just the way we are?

Love being the great phenomena that it is though, why do we so resist? For some, it has to do with comfort zones. Comfort zones are great for providing us with comfort or a good playing field suitable for the way *we* play or *our* game. To step into another's space though requires being in *their* space. Unless their space is the same as yours, you must step into theirs. This requires leaving your space, comfort zone(s). The beauty is, it also requires them leaving their space, if necessary. One of the primary reasons for relationship failures may be the investment in someone who will not come to where we are, and to whom we will not go. Stepping out with no good destination can be just as digressive as staying in the zone, or even worse. If either one of us is not headed for love, one of us will miss it and end up somewhere else.

Perhaps, both parties are best served with *some* similarities, especially if they have no intention of growing (leaving their comfort zones), or being challenged. If you're both couch potatoes, have a swell time on the couch *together*! But if she just loves hiking and he sits there, it could be an issue. Of course there are other people to hike with. But if it is *that* important, it could be a great divide. Especially if she's vulnerable to the hot hiking buddy who totally knocks her socks off. Vice versa. Yes, we shouldn't suggest that he finds an attractive *couch* potato buddy. Vulnerabilities, you see. If you're over having a fling with the other buddy, maybe you can handle another buddy besides your significant other. Where will it lead? Most of us are a little too vulnerable for such scenarios.

To define love to be what is comfortable for us does not make it love. Most of our love explanations make it our perception of love. And if we continue to do that, we will continue to have what we have - hearts requiring another to bend to its sway, at least a billion hearts in their own corner.

Love has a "table". If we all come to love's table, we are on the same page. And this entity that has so much power can infect and affect the human race with its grand influence. If we were considering some foul arena (hate, maybe), it would be most sensible not to come. But when such a positively powerful principle invites us to opulence, why do we not R.S.V.P., come, but with no intentions of releasing our hang ups and impediments, or not come at all?

To accept love's invitation sincerely, we should be open to relinquishing totally our own perspectives of love. To come any other way, is to hamper our efforts to become. So powerful is love, in cooperating with it, it can direct, guide and regroup the heart. And hence, a fear. We hold *our* truths to be so dear. They have created and shaped our world. Whatever success or destination, we've arrived because of what, and who, we think we are. How to do life without the crutches? Walk free. Is that habit or behavior freeing or limiting. The freedom of love empowers.

How did you form that opinion or the other? How did you get in *that* comfort zone? What exactly drove you there? Was it an experience, an event, a journey or just your own deliberate choice? For even our own deliberate choices are grounded in something. If they're not based on love then they are an obstacle to becoming love. And, if we don't know what love is, we most certainly have some decisions, opinions and beliefs that are not love-based. Where do we want to go?

CAKE. ... AND, EAT IT TOO.

Who doesn't like some kind of cake? ... So many varieties and decadences. Even the no-sweet-toother can find something to tickle their delightful cake pleasure. Any flavor of ice-cream or sorbet cakes included, surely you can find one right up your alley. For some of us though, cake is a direct route to overindulgence of the grossest kind. If you ever stole a piece of cake or sweet treat (as a child), the adventure was somehow soooo… edgy! Oh, and don't let it happen that you got away with it! Welcome to the world of *more*. More cake, more treats, more underhanded sneaking an opportunity and letting the temptation be your guide. Whatever your cake, the point is overindulgence and the temptation to have the tantalizingly pleasureful; usually, out of our league!

For the most part, who does not want their cake and eat it too? If we can have what we want, why do what love or anyone else wants? The stance of *the* wife and the flings is such an ideal place. The problem is nobody with love aspirations wants to play. So, some bow to the fact that most will not play *that* game, and look in the direction of love. But the idealism of what they think they really want is still somewhere on the back or front burner. There is limited place for love with other relationship flings and things burning up on the back burner and elsewhere. If we can have flings and things, most of us will have that over some unnatural development of the lifestyle of love. Many of us insist that our fling-type relationships and personal love style are really *it*.

Unfortunately, love does not change what it is to suit our interpretations of it: interpretations that are geared to what we need love to be in all of our diverse situations, every day. We continue to require that love become something that we've created it to be. And worse than that, we expect others to come to our perception, and live it with us. A premium consideration of love is, it is a great common ground. If you meet her there, you can play free. If you meet him there, love is what you have. The more time we spend in our own corners, the less we will become love, and live one of the truest, and most powerful, phenomena we have the capacity to enjoy.

Love being designated a quality that accepts one as is, why require anything more? Is love *"acceptance"* the way we have defined it to be though? If love desires the best good for someone, how does love leave him as he is? Can he come to a place of love? How do you call him there? The finesse of love is its ability to bring one to love places without them even knowing they came. That's power. If you don't have that, be cautious of dragging her there, kicking and screaming. Love can finesse us all we want, if we're not going, then *there* is where we will stay. And love accepts us right where we are. It will always desire our best good, but knows us enough to know if we can, or even want to, go there. Everyone can get there. Everyone doesn't want to go. So many of us *want* to go, but lack the will to go, and we're not giving our power away - not even to love. Trust issues, you see. Big problem – because inherent in love is trust. The vicious cycle.

We don't trust love so refuse to embrace it. If we do not embrace it, we cannot have it. Love is one place where you can totally let your guard down, drop your crutches, lean fully, and still be free. Make sure it's love. - not her bed. If you think love to be the boudoir thing, keep the crutches until you meet love - in your face, bold, real love. Don't approach the fakes, throwing yourself mercilessly at them. Mistaken love is quite common. Again, it has to do with perspective.   If our perception or definition of love is false, we tend to get burned. It is vital to be open to what love really is. But, if we hold on with knuckles white and purple like a vice grip to what love is not, we cannot possibly have love.

The fruit of love cannot help but produce beauty and life. It's worth eating. Eat love cake. This is one area of overindulgence that's very good for you. But first we must get it. The life nourished with love has an entirely different capacity than the love malnourished one. Be *deliberate* about love! When the deliberate and conscious decision is made to do love, and nothing else, one has a much better chance of being love.

WHAT'S YOUR MOTIVATION?

What's in it for *me*? Oh yeah! Gimme *something*! We work, we get money. We exercise, we get buff (fit). We sleep, we get rejuved. We love, we get … What? The love thing is so misrepresented, many of us think: we love, we get hurt, divorced, tied up with a bunch of principles that guilt us, … We love, we get vulnerable.

It's not ideal being at the mercy of. Especially at the mercy of that which causes stress. If love's stressing you out, make sure it's love, and work with it. It's one thing to be presented with a challenge. It takes savvy to work it to your advantage. Work love to your advantage. Love is advantageous in and of itself, but if adapting to it goes against your grain, step back and find ways to make it work for you. If she loves you, she will do anything for you that is in your best interest. That's incentive. Most of us are not necessarily drawn nor guided by principles, unless it will make us the next million, or feed our libido. A life of principles does not appeal to the masses. There are some above averages who want love. The real thing, not the stress.

Are we giving up, or just completely on the wrong path of approaching love? The divorce headline is a constant. Even after so many years of marriage or living together, people get divorced or break up. Some, not quite years. Some of us don't really have the interest to "make it work". Who's really into love? Until we see love with power to decide our bank accounts, or get us what we want, it's a side issue for many of us.

It is even instinctive to want family, kids, the dog, the house or the other bells and whistles. After many get it, it's okay to move on. It's like graduation from high school. Who wants to stay in high school all their life? When we've achieved what we think one relationship can give us, why stay? One of the problems with this is, you can't invest in something without, at least, emotional, tangible or non-tangible fallouts, if it fails. We get personal about our financial investments that don't pan out, but get what we think we want from our human relations and walk off. Science has yet to present such emotional tolls on our health comprehensively and conclusively, but we cannot affect the heart without somehow affecting other aspects of our lives.

The lovestruck that is about love, just for love, is rare, and can be somewhat unpopular. What are you bringing to the table? Beauty and brains are hardly the stuff of commitment. He did that with the first one. And, while money may still be an attractive draw, it's best to not come to the table to play with his money or hers. What do you have that is so vitally important to him, he can't live without it? What do have that makes you her must-have? If it's not ultimately *you*, what is it? Is what you have that she cannot live without relationally sustainable? Emotionals and high maintenance emotionals can be very taxing and counterproductive to lover status.

In a world where we have what we want, love gets lost. The irony is we're still searching for it, or falling in and out of it. It seems "love" must have a twist that feeds the fancy. Love *can* be very dramatic, but is that love though? If drama is what we want, love has that too, but there's a difference between the melodramatics of love and Broadway. It is best to spare the hearts, and go to the show if we're not game for love. As dramatic as love can be, the drama is about you, and motivated from what love is, the real deal.

If we could get just a slight glimpse of the potential of our lives with ultimate love, we'd stop selling ourselves short. Settling hearts attract the same to places of debilitating mediocrity. We become so lost in the dailies of life, relationships sink downhill into the quagmire of hearts so far apart, reconciliation doesn't even enter the equation.

How much of our humanity are we losing with our casual approach to divorces, separation, broken and toxic relationships? The colors of our relationships and hearts tell the story of where we are. Most people want good love relationships, but get lost in stuck, and sometimes tired, places. Tired of being the one doing all of the doing, tired of being unappreciated, tired of, … The quandary is a vast majority still want love,… or something.

Why do people do the marriage thing anymore? If it is love, why doesn't it work? Inherent in love is staying the course. Not abuse places, but relationship places. How does leaving because it is not beneficial to us love, or not love? Is it that we love *ourselves* way too much to stay and work things out? But if he or she is not making sense in light of *what we want them to be*, why continue trying to make sense of nonsense? Ultimately, and sorry to say, if love is really what we want, love works it out. If she is unwilling to work it out, how does love stay and be the superior power that it is? Can it turn a heart? Love does not give up. O, how very daunting, but love stays the course.

Many leave only to meet similar encounters and failures. Moving on requires answering the question, "Will I work *this* out with someone else?" As long as you're breathing and moving on, if love is anywhere remotely into you, it will require of your heart. So the mess you left back there, will be where you're going, possibly repackaged, if you don't work it out. Eventually, you still have to front yourself. (Front: confront). Perhaps you will be willing to confront yourself for someone else. But if you want good relationships, you will have to address you.

Is *she* sexier? The other woman. Does he pay more attention to you or *her*? If our dysfunctional relationships, infidelities, break-ups, separations and divorces are considered truthfully, we may have grounds to regroup better relationally. If it's a sexy thing, should he find the sexiest and make it happen? If he found the sexiest woman alive for the current relationship, how does he explain the split? If we choose who is best, why the splits? And if who we have is best, why move on to someone "lesser"? How will it be different from what you had? Are *you* better? And if best doesn't work, is it that best is not good enough, or you were not satisfied? So many questions! If we can start over, and go forward without trips, falls, and detriment, the analyses are irrelevant. Unfortunately, forward does not eliminate roots, habits and relationship killers, unless we are proactive and deliberate about us.

Can we be satisfied? What does it take to satisfy a species that is ever seeking for *more*? What is this dilemma (cannot be satisfied) on the scale of our infidelities and splits? Upon moving on to Relationship F, are we satisfied with F or still searching? By the time we've done A-F, does something click somewhere in our subconscious that our quest is more than a significant other relationship thing? Change requires adaptability. We can be very dynamic about business, economy and other trends, but somehow remain stuck when we need to transition to maintain love relationships. It speaks of how we value the most precious "commodity", him or her.

If we really hope to come to some resolve on the love thing, honesty is critical. It is futile to spend ourselves asking questions which we haven't the courage to answer truthfully. If all we want is to circle our relationship problems, they will remain. If we really want to do love to the extent of embracing love, dive into truth about love, and most irrefutably, about ourselves.

LOVE: SHE HAS A WAY ABOUT HER

The lover is in you. Do you suppress him with half-stepping love antics or let her unleash? How ironic that that which our soul really craves, we think we have so little capacity to acquire and be. But acquiring a taste for love, like anything else "unpalatable", requires some commitment of the will. Whether we can decipher it with the heart or mind, ultimately, the life wants love. When we walk away from the current relationship or the next fling, no matter how wounded (or rich), our life will still want love. Perhaps that is, in part, why we inevitably desire or seek another relationship. We are driven by the soul of us, more or less independent of our will, for that which our life instinctively craves.

No matter how buried our soul, it ultimately wants love.   And yes, it wants the real McCoy. Not our renditions. This is one of the reasons why we are not satisfied with our relationships. Because the life really wants "real" love that satisfies the life. Life: that which makes us *alive*!

The most extreme vacations, dream homes and surreal performances leave the soul gaping, still. What the soul finds entertaining is just entertaining. It is not love. If he loves like that or she does, quite naturally, the soul is so inclined to him or her. However, it can tell a fake or a façade.

If your conquests were exorbitant wealth, a hundred women and power, your life would still crave love if at least one of them did not possess it. While we can separate physically, mentally and emotionally from our self to engage in whatever affairs, the soul is guided by love. It will ever be uneasy, unsettled or lost without it. And when we collect ourselves from the distractions, the soul is still there longing for what will consume it to quiet satisfaction.

To adapt love's ways requires an embracing of the soul's innate desire for love, and living the ways of love. For the most part, most of our lives are not conducive to love's ways. We've learned how to turn up the volume to drown out the aching of love. The music does fade, the lights go down and the show ends.

The profound beauty of love is that its ways are dedicated to our best good. Our life even knows when we haven't the will to pursue love. Lives that have mastered the art of covering up learn to forego the ways of love for more familiar paths. But, O the heart that aspires to love. In it lies the secret to woo lovers, direct influence and impact economies.

The soul craves love because love feeds its life. There are no substitutes. Hence the hunger that persists after trying to quench with inadequate means. If the soul is deprived of love, it will ever scream above the lesser fillers. The fakes haven't the essentials to satisfy such an appetite. For one of the life's most prime foods is love. Whether we can "make it" or not without love is not the discussion here. We can make it without many things. It is quality of life of which we speak. A life rich in material wealth and resources is a shrivel if it is starved of love. And, even what *seems* to be love cannot beguile the life. So we continue to come back to old places, or find new ones. Not necessarily just because we're bored or the familiars don't work. The driver of the life is malnourished or dying. It will ever require of us. And when the fillers are no longer adequate, the soul will still be there – aching, vital, calling.

Just because love is not as quantifiable as bank, does not mean it hasn't immeasurable value. It is a disservice to use a metric that does not fit. Perhaps our best measurement of the richness of love is evident in the hearts that have embraced it, and even more unmistakably clear in the lives that live so without it. To bring the human race to hearts that aspire to love is to change every dynamic that we have to greatness. And, if we think that we are "well-of", rich or complete, you should see us if love is our driver.

How does the heart know when it has found love? The life most familiar with love, just inherently knows.

AUTHOR PAGE

Milan Ester writes to challenge us to love, to believe in love and seek love. Her goal is to be practical about us, about relationships and about life with us or with a significant other. Success – money, love, personal – is just a fringe benefit of a life that is wealthy in love, in love resources.